Strategy

JACOB VARGHESE

AuthorHouse™
1663 Liberty Drive
Bloomington, IN 47403
www.authorhouse.com
Phone: 1-800-839-8640

© 2012 by Jacob Varghese. All rights reserved.

No part of this book may be reproduced, stored in a retrieval system, or transmitted by any means without the written permission of the author.

Published by AuthorHouse   04/13/2012

ISBN: 978-1-4685-8094-5 (sc)
ISBN: 978-1-4685-8093-8 (e)

Library of Congress Control Number: 2012906899

Any people depicted in stock imagery provided by Thinkstock are models, and such images are being used for illustrative purposes only.
Certain stock imagery © Thinkstock.

This book is printed on acid-free paper.

Because of the dynamic nature of the Internet, any web addresses or links contained in this book may have changed since publication and may no longer be valid. The views expressed in this work are solely those of the author and do not necessarily reflect the views of the publisher, and the publisher hereby disclaims any responsibility for them.

Table of Contents

Introduction ix
1.0 Task Environment: 1
    1.0.1 Defining the link between
    Environmental Analysis to Industry Analysis 1
    1.1 The Determinants of Industry Profit:
    demand and competition 2
    1.2 Structural Analysis 3
    1.3 Porter's five Forces of Competition Framework 5
    1.3.1 The Five Forces shaping Strategy 6
    1.3.2 Applying Industry Analysis 6
    1.4 Strategies to alter Industry Structure or freedom to manoeuvre ... 7
    1.4.1 Regarding strategic Manoeuvring: 7
    1.5 Porter generic strategies. 7
    1.5.1 Cost leadership 8
Marketing strategy 9
Competitive advantage 10
Profitability and customer loyalty through Low cost position : 10
Using low cost position for superior business performance 10
    1.5.2 Differentiation 11
Marketing strategy 12
Competitive advantage 12
    1.5.2.2 Differentiation strategy 12
Strategic Positioning through
Economics of scale 2.0 Five forces,
rivalry and the demand related strategic P's 12
Formations of perceptions and preferences 14
    2.3 Stage 3: Alternative evaluation 14
    2.3.1 Perceptions. 14
    2.3.2 Perceptions of products /beliefs about products: 15
    2.3.3 The usefulness of perception 15

Barrier to entry	16
2.5 Instrumental or functional attributes	16
Supplier power	16
Threat of Rivalry	17
2.5.2 (Fixed cost/ Value added	17
Barrier to entry	17
Threat of substitutes	18
2.5.4 Relative Price Performance of substitutes:	18
2.6.1 Buyer power	19
Supplier power	19
Threat of Rivalry	19
2.6.3 Diverse Competitors	19
Threat of substitutes	20
Barrier to entry	20
Barrier to entry	21
2.7.1 Market Breadth:	21
Strategic Repositioning through economics of scope.	22
3.1 Stage2: what benefits do the consumers and /or buyers want?	22
3.2.1 The method for employing the technique	24
Consumer's preference function	25
Barrier to entry:	25
Supplier power	25
Threat of Rivalry	26
Barrier to entry	27
Barrier to entry	28
Buyer power	28
Threat of substitutes	28
The economic logic of Market segmentation analysis	29
3.6.3.2 The advantages of achieving customer value through economics of scope	29

   3.7 Attitude or utility 29
       3.7.1 Fish bein–Rosenberg model 30
       3.8 Subsequent stages in the decision process. 30
       3.8.5 Expected costs 31
Reference Books 35
Journals 37
Working paper 40
Internet sources 41
Abbreviations 43
Illustrations 43

Introduction

Task environment[1]

Firm success is manifested in attaining a competitive position or series of competitive positions that leads to a superior and sustainable financial performance. Michael porter integrated three key areas of analysis-Industry analysis, competitor analysis, and industry evolution analysis-to form a comprehensive new model of competitive industry analysis.

Positioning school[2]
Michael Porter focused more systematically on external forces and the changing nature of competition within the Industry to which the firm belongs. "The five forces "belong to the "Positioning school", widely known as the Porters Five forces model. Porter's model of competitive analysis became the dominant strategy approach and continues to be a strong force in business education today. The name positioning school stems from Porter's central idea that a business should try to achieve 'competitiveness through positioning' and to enhance financial performance. Positioning determines whether a firm's profitability is above or below the industry average. The basic assumption is that the industry environment largely determines the firm's freedom to manoeuvre. The environment has far more influence in shaping firms' strategies than the other way around; a company should place more emphasis on adapting to the environment .Since the underlying logic of the positioning approach is to

---

[1] Porter, 1991
[2] Volberda and Elfring, 2001

first understand the external environment (Environmental Scanning)and next to position the firm, it is also referred to as the outside –in approach.

Business performance[3] (Domain of financial + Operational Performance) measures market related items such as Market share,growth, New Product development & diversification. There appears to be two dimensions here a) Those indicators related to growth/share in existing business and b) those indicators related to future positioning of the firm. The Resource based and the competence-based view argues that the firm should be aligned to its environment. In the resource –based and the competence –based view. however, the method for arriving at this alignment or [4]strategic fit puts more emphasis on the strength of the firm (and thus its resources and competencies and the possibility of creating its own environment . In highly dynamic environments ,management can commit resources to an idea in which they believe a market can be created by unbundling products and unbundling the current value chains, new products, new ways of doing business, new markets emerge. Based on prior research[5] there are two strategic orientations.Strategic scope and strategic posture, which are independent to each other. Preserving the long time future of the firm pushes the firm to reconsider its strategic posture and its strategic scope. Based on prior research there are two strategic orientations . Strategic

---

[3] Gray,1997
[4] Mintzberg 1994
[5] Houthofeed and heene,1997

scope and strategic posture, which are independent to each other. Preserving the long time future of the firm pushes the firm to reconsider its strategic posture and its strategic scope. Demand considerations are expressly entertained by the focus on finding and satisfying the needs, tastes or customer values, and Customer preferences of particular customer segments. The key element in Managing for the long time future is the readiness to periodically reframe the dominant logic[6] about the rent generating perspective of Strategic scope dimensions are Buyer diversity, Product variety, Geographical reach & vertical integration/disintegration - strategic posture dimensions(Innovation, risktaking, Proactiveness) in the future. Firms with widely varying Strategic postures can be equally Profitable .Segmentation provides an excellent analytical tool for determining which of these strategies will lead to profitable growth. The most profitable strategies will be those that target customer segments that ascribe the highest relative value to the firms unique products and service. .Segmentation strategy is viable in markets where customer value is premised more on tastes and preferences than on price, where different groups of customers exist in a market, and where the economics of scope predominate the economics of scale within the market. In this types of markets, growth strategies based on customer segmentation offer feasible opportunities to deliver profitable growth through differentiated competitive position.Utility- The way the product is perceived in terms of the various attributes in one hand and the preferential weights on the other

---

[6] prahalad & bettis 1986

hand are measured using the Fishbone Rosenberg model. Decision process- internal resource analysis determines the resource requirements necessary to support the customer value where functional capability,and resource analysis and value chain analysis will be the helpful tools to conduct the internal scrutiny. Outcome -This analysis determines an extremely refined definition of exactly what customers in each segment value.

1.0 Task Environment:

Beyond managing dimensions of the internal environment system, technologically competitive firms must strategically position themselves to task environment influences. Firms are embedded in various contextual matrices[1], which most immediately include the specific industry competitive dynamics, or task environment)[2], and the global competitive environment[3]. Both of these environments include competitors, customers, regulators, supplier relationships, substitutes, and entry and exit barriers. Depending on the specific situation, each of these factors may have a direct impact on the value-added creation processes.

Research has demonstrated that companies in some environments can gain an advantage over their competition based on the quality of their environmental analysis[4].

1.0.1 Defining the link between Environmental Analysis to Industry Analysis[5]

The business environment of the firm consists of all the external influences that affect its decisions and performance. Given the vast number of external influences. It stands as a big

---

[1] Miller & Friesen 1977; Grinyer & Norburn, 1977/78.Pg 99-122
[2] Thompson(1967) pg,27
[3] L.C. Rhyne et al,2002 Pg 254
[4] Miller & Friesen, 1977; Grinyer & Norburn, 1977/78.Pg 99-122
[5] Industry analysis : The fundamentalsc5A5eco381).pdf Pg 68

challenge for Managers to monitor environmental conditions. The starting point of framework for organising information.

The prerequisite for effective environmental analysis is to distinguish the vital from the merely important.

The First principles for the firm to make profit are to make value for customers. Hence, it must understand customers.

Second, in creating value, the firm acquires goods and services from suppliers. Hence, it must understand its suppliers and how to form to form business relationships with them.

Third, the ability to generate profitability from value-creating activity depends on the intensity of competition among firms that vie for the same value-creating opportunities. Hence, the firm must understand competition. Thus, the core of the firm's business environment is formed by its relationships with three sets of players: customers, suppliers, and competitors. This is the Industry environment

1.1 The Determinants of Industry Profit: demand and competition[6]

Business is about the creation of value for the customer either by production (transforming inputs into outputs) or commerce (arbritage).

---

[6] Industry analysis: The fundamentalsc5A5eco381).pdf Pg 73

Value is created when the price the customer is willing to pay for a product exceeds the costs incurred by the firm. but value creation does not translate directly into profit. The surplus of value over the cost is distributed between customers and producers by the forces of competition.

The stronger is competition among producers, the more of the surplus is received by customers in consumer surplus and the less is the surplus received by the producer. The surplus by producers over and above the minimum cost of production is not entirely captured in profits. A substantial part of the surplus may be appropriated by these suppliers (employees united by a strong labour union)

The profits earned by the firms in an industry are thus determined by three factors.
1. a) The value of the product to customers,
2. b) The intensity of competition
3. c) The bargaining power of the producers relative to their suppliers.

Industry analysis brings all three factors into a single analytic framework

1.2 Structural Analysis

Structural analysis of industries, the five forces model with the forces bargaining power of suppliers and buyers, the threat of new entrants and substitute products, and rivalry among existing firms. The five-force framework is then used to identify the three generic competitive strategies to achieve a defendable competitive position. Companies may choose to compete based on lower cost aiming at a mass market and understanding the competition or they may decide to follow a differentiation strategy aimed at broad market[7].

A firm that can position it well may earn high rates of return even though industry structure is unfavourable and the average profitability of the industry is modest. The fundamental basis of above average performance in the long run is sustainable competitive advantage. There are two basic types of competitive advantage a firm can process: low cost or differentiation[8]. The Significance of any strength or weakness a firm possesses is ultimately a function of its impact on relative cost or differentiation. The two basic types of competitive advantage combined with the scope of activities for which a firm seeks to achieve them, lead to three generic strategies: Cost leadership, differentiation and focus.

Focus Strategies which is one that concentrates on a particular geographic or demographic market and attempts to serve only this niche, to the exclusion of others[9]

---

[7] WP data/IPCWEB/MSWORD/WP-9MS.Doc.(March 1994) Pg 1-19
[8] WP data/IPCWEB/MSWORD/WP-9MS.Doc.(March 1994)
[9] WP data/IPCWEB/MSWORD/WP-9MS.Doc.(March 1994)

1.3 Porter's five Forces of Competition Framework[10]

These five forces of competition include three sources of" horizontal" competition: competition from substitutes, competition from Potential entrants, and competition from established rivals; and two sources of "vertical "competition: The bargaining power of suppliers and buyers. The strength of each of these competitive forces is determined by a number of key structural variables.

Once the forces affecting competition in an industry and their underlying cause has been diagnosed, the firm is in a position to identify its strength and weakness relative to the industry. The crucial strength & weaknesses are the firm's posture (Maintaining and improving profitability) underlying the causes of each competitive force:

- Positioning the firm so that its capabilities provide the defence against existing array of competitive forces;
- Influencing the balance of forces through strategic moves, hereby improving the firm's relative position.

Anticipating shifts in the factors underlying the forces and responding to them, hereby exploiting change by choosing a strategy appropriate to the new competitive balance before rivals recognise it.

---

[10] Industry analysis:. The fundamentalsc5A5eco381).pdf Pg 73

1.3.1 The Five Forces shaping Strategy[11]

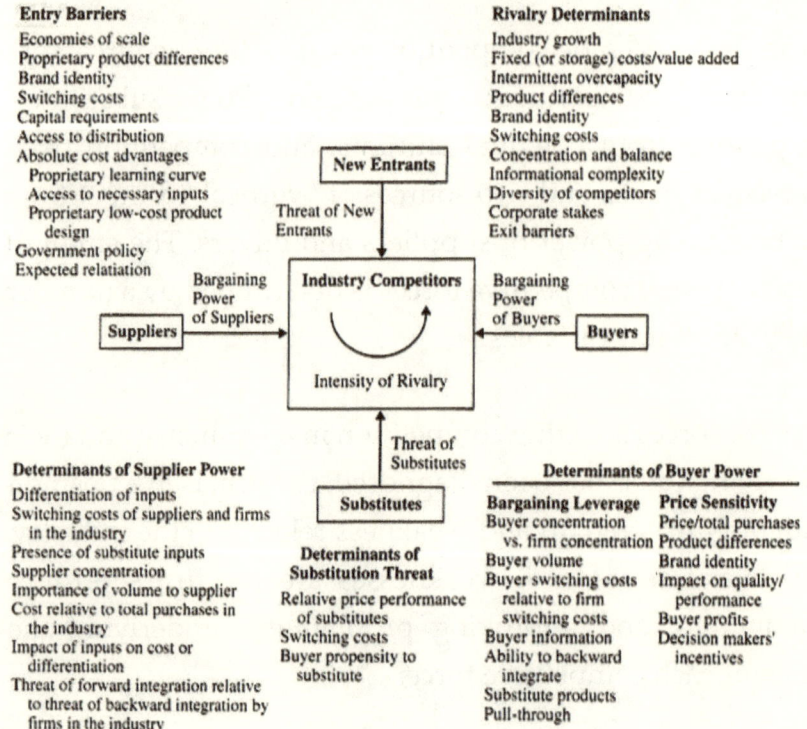

1.3.2 Applying Industry Analysis

Once we understand how industry structure drives competition. Which, in turn, determines industry profitability, we can apply this analysis. First to forecasting industry profitability in the future, and second to devising strategies for changing industry structure.

---

[11] Porter & Montgomery.1991 Pg 12

1.4 Strategies to alter Industry Structure or freedom to manoeuvre

Understanding how the structural characteristics of an Industry determine the intensity of competition and level of profitability provides a basis for identifying opportunities for changing industry structure in order to alleviate competitive pressures. The first issue is to identify the key structural features of an industry that are responsible for depressing profitability. The second is to consider which of these structural features are amenable to change through appropriate strategic initiatives.

Along these lines goals and decisions emerge from bargaining, negotiation, and jockeying for position among different stake holder[12].

1.4.1 Regarding strategic Manoeuvring[13]:

Many moves that would significantly improve a firm's position do threaten competitors . . . . . Thus a key success . . . is predicting and influencing retaliation.

1.5 Porter generic strategies[14].

Michael Porter assesses strategy on the dimensions of strategic scope and strategic strength. Strategic scope refers to the breadth of the market penetration while strategic strength refers to the firm's sustainable competitive advantage

---

[12] Bolman and Deal, 1997 Pg 163
[13] Porter,1980.Pg 91
[14] www.Encyclopedia.lockergnome.com/s/b/experience_curve_effect

A firm can achieve profitability[15] over a rival in two fundamentally different approaches to business strategy either differentiation or cost leadership. Differentiation and cost leadership are mutually exclusive strategies

1.5.1 Cost leadership[16]
In a cost leadership strategy a firm sets out to become the low-cost producer in its branch. The sources of low cost producer must find and exploit all sources of cost advantage. If a firm can achieve and sustain overall cost leadership, then it will be an above average performer provided it could command prices at the average. At equivalent or lower prices than its rivals.

Some of the ways that firms acquire cost advantages are by improving process efficiencies, gaining unique access to large source of lower cost materials, making optimal outsourcing and vertical integration decisions, or avoiding some costs altogether. If competing firms are unable to lower their costs by a similar amount, the firm may be able to sustain a competitive advantage based on cost leadership.

Firms that succeed in cost leadership often have the following internal strengths[17]:
1) Access to Capital required making a significant investment in production assets; this investment

---

[15] Porter 1980,1985
[16] P.Gibcus, R.G.M Kemp, 2003 Pg 18
[17] www.quickmba.com/strategy/generic.shtml.

represents a barrier to entry that many firms may not overcome.
2) Skill in designing products for efficient manufacturing, for example, having a small component count to shorten the assembly process.
3) High level of expertise in manufacturing process engineering.
4) Efficient distribution.

Marketing strategy

1.5.1.1 Aggressiveness

Is concerned with the interaction between an organization and its competitors. The variable reflects degree of competitiveness (or competitive posture) in relations with competing organizations. Early PIMS studies[18] (e.g., prescriptions grounded in the growth-share matrix[19] and generic cost leadership strategy [20]emphasize the importance of aggressiveness in seeking Market share. This aggressiveness or competitive orientation is described as "attack strategies" aimed at increasing market share. and sacrificing profit or spending aggressively compared to competitors on marketing, product & Service quality and capacity[21]. It also reflects a willingness to be unconventional, rather following traditional methods of competing(radical innovation).

---

[18] Porter,1980 Pg 35
[19] Porter 1980 Pg 36
[20] Porter,1980 Pg 36
[21] Buzzell, Gale, and Sultan 1975 Pg 97-106

Competitive advantage

1.5.1.2 Cost strategy[22]

Cost leadership requires aggressive construction of efficient—scale facilities, vigorous pursuit of cost reductions from experience, tight cost and overhead control, avoidance of marginal customer accounts, and cost minimisation in areas like R & D, service, sales force, and advertising and so on.

Profitability and customer loyalty through Low cost position [23]:

- Implementing the low cost strategy may require heavy up front capital investments in the state of art equipment, aggressive pricing, and start up losses to build market share.
- High Market share may in turn allow economics in purchasing which lower costs even further.

Once achieved, the low cost position provides high margins which can be reinvested in new equipment and modern facilities in order to maintain cost leadership. Such reinvestment may well be a prerequisite to sustaining a low cost position.

Using low cost position for superior business performance

Achieving a low overall cost position often requires a high relative market share or other advantages, or favourable access to raw materials. It may well require designing products for

---

[22] MacMillan 1982
[23] Porter, 1980 Pg 35

ease in manufacturing, maintaining a wide line of related products to spread costs, and serving all major customer groups in order to build volume

1.5.2 Differentiation

In a differentiation strategy, a firm seeks to be unique along some dimensions that are highly valued by buyers. It seeks one or more attributes than many buyers in an industry perceive as important and uniquely positions it to meet those needs. It is rewarded for its uniqueness with a premium price. Differentiation can be based on product itself, the delivery system by which it is sold, the marketing approach and a broad range of other factors. A firm that can achieve and sustain differentiation will be an above-average performer[24] in its industry if its price premium exceeds the extra costs. Incurred in being unique. A differentiator, therefore, must always seek ways of differentiating that lead to a price premium greater than the cost of differentiating. In order to do so, the firm needs resources and distinctive competencies that can create a sustainable competitive advantage

Firms that succeed in differentiation strategy often have the following internal strengths[25]:

1.) Access to leading scientific research.
2.) Highly skilled and creative product development team.
3.) Strong sales team with the ability to successfully communicate the perceived strength of the product.

---

[24] Postma and Zwart,2001
[25] www.quickmba.com/strategy/generic.shtml

4.) Corporate reputation for quality and innovation.

Marketing strategy

1.5.2.1 Specialisation
Focuses on the interaction between an organisation and its customers. It reflects to the extent to which a business attempts to create a unique product (or set of products) that is perceived by consumers as clearly superior in value. Specialisation, general termed differentiation, has been suggested as a key strategy dimension in the marketing[26], business policy and Industrial organisation economics literature.

Competitive advantage

1.5.2.2 Differentiation strategy
Achieving differentiation will imply a trade off[27] with cost position if the activities required in creating it are inherently costly, such as extensive research, product design, high quality materials, or intensive customer support

---

[26] Gorton T.Gray Pg 1-11
[27] Evans & Wurster,1997 Pg 4

Strategic Positioning through Economics of scale 2.0

Five forces, rivalry and the demand related strategic P's[28]

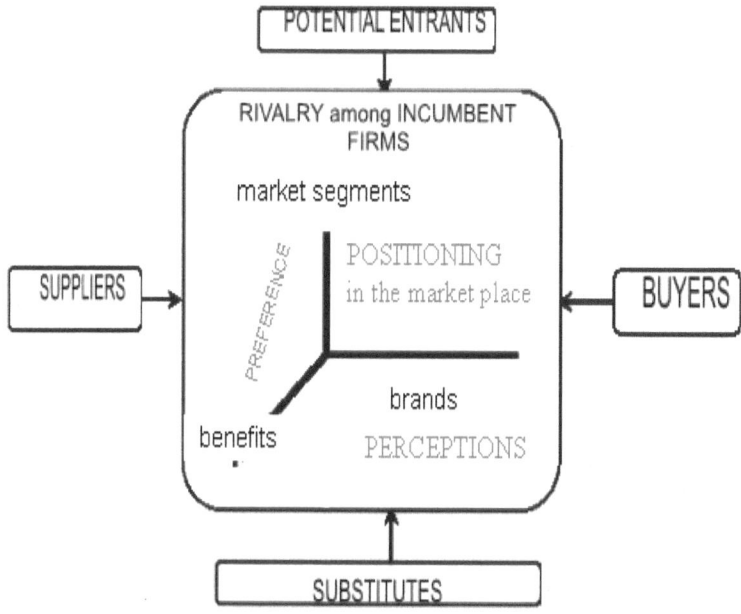

2.1 Stage1: Deals with the physiological needs

As Hunger, thirst or observation of products in shops, advertisements or elsewhere, the consumer has somehow become involved in a problem of choice.

2.2 Stage2: Refers to the information seeking activity[29]

Of the consumer before he makes his choice. If the consumers are purchasing a low cost good. They may not opt for total

---

[28] Houthooofd Noel and Heene, 2000 Pg 7
[29] Wieranga B 1983 Pg 122

Market information indicating that the supplier can dictate terms to the consumer, but if the product represents a relatively large expense for the consumer. They will have access for total Market information as market demand/prices of goods. There will be less room for negotiations and in such cases the buyer or consumer will have the bargaining power.

Formations of perceptions and preferences[30]

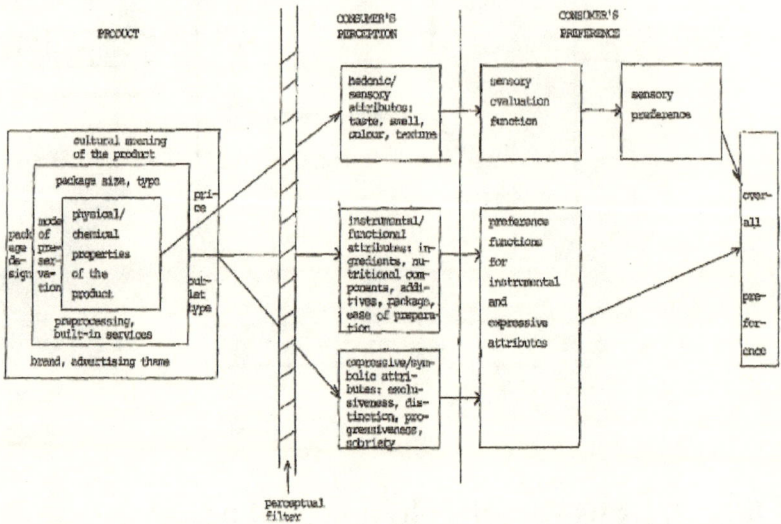

2.3 Stage 3: Alternative evaluation

2.3.1 Perceptions.
The relevant perceptual dimensions and the beliefs of the consumer with respect to the performance of the product on the relevant dimensions

---

[30] Wieranga B 1983 Pg 124

2.3.2 Perceptions of products /beliefs about products[31]:

This refers to the way products are seen by the consumer.e.g., product attributes. Since consumers often have imperfect information, perception of products may well differ from objective reality. Perceptions are formed by information and experience.

2.3.3 The usefulness of perception

This result in an overall utility or an attitude with respect to the various alternative choices. In principle, he will choose the alternative with the greatest utility and this choice leads to a certain outcome: the satisfaction obtained from the product chosen[32]. In general model of consumer decision—making It is customary to distinguish 5 stages in the decision process: (1)problem recognition (2),search (3),Alternative evaluation (4),Choice and (5) Outcome

2.4 Hedonic attributes[33]

These attributes are related to feelings of joy, pleasure and delight in consuming the product. Hedonic attributes refer to aspects such as taste, smell, flavour, i.e. the sensory aspects of a product

---

[31] Simon,1967 Pg 29-39
[32] Wieranga B 1983 Pg 122
[33] Wieranga B 1983 127

Barrier to entry

2.4.1 Favourable access to raw materials[34] established firms may have locked up the most favourable sources and /or tied up foreseeable needs at prices reflecting a lower demand for them than currently exists.

2.5 Instrumental or functional attributes[35]

Attributes such as ingredients, contents of specific nutritional components, types of components, presence/absence of additives can be classified as instrumental or functional e.g. Package size, ease of preparation, quality etc.

Supplier power

2.5.1 Supplier concentration[36]: It is dominated by a few companies and is more than the industry it sells to. Suppliers selling to more fragmented buyers will usually be able to exert considerable influence in process, quality and terms.

2.5.1.1 Cost position relative to supplier concentration[37] Low cost position defends the firm against powerful buyers because buyers can exert power only to drive down prices to the level of the next efficient competitor.

---

[34] Porter 1980 Pg 11
[35] Wieranga B 1983 127
[36] Porter 1980 Pg 27
[37] Porter 1980 Pg 36

Threat of Rivalry

2.5.2 (Fixed cost/ Value added [38]

There are high fixed costs of production. When a large percentage of the cost to produce products is independent of the number of units produced, businesses are pressured to produce large volumes. This may tempt companies to drastically cut prices when there is excess capacity in the industry for order.

2.5.2.1 Cost relative to Industry competitors[39]. A low cost provides a defense against powerful suppliers by providing more flexibility to cope with cost increases

Barrier to entry

2.5.3 Units of Multi business[40] may reap economics similar to those of scale if they are able to share operations or functions subject to economics of scale with other businesses in the company. Thus related diversification around common operations or functions can remove volume constraints imposed by the size of the industry.

---

[38] Porter 1980 Pg 8 & 11
[39] Porter 1980 Pg 36
[40] Porter 1980, Pg 9

Threat of substitutes

2.5.4 Relative Price Performance of substitutes: [41]

Customers have little loyalty. When price is the consumer's primary motivator the threat of substitution is greater.

2.5.4.1 Low cost relative to substitutes[42]: A low cost position usually places the firm in a favorable position vis-à-vis substitute relative to its competitors in the industry.

2.6.0 Strategic groups[43] are groups of firms that pursue similar types of strategies within the same industry. Strategic groups exist because of strong economic forces acting within an Industry that constrain firms from easily switching from one competitive posture or position to another. Firms within each strategic group might be similar to one another in terms of any number of different key attributes, such as

1.) Product line breadth,
2.) Type of technology us

2.6.0.1 Strategic group advantages: The presence of groups[44] within an Industry moderates the amount of rivalry at Industry level. The rivalry between groups is more intense

---

[41] Cloe ehmke, Joan Fulton, and Jay Akridge Pg 10
[42] Porter 1980 Pg 36
[43] Houthoofd,N & Heene, A1997 Pg. 429-451
[44] Porter,1979: Pg.218

than rivalry within groups because opportunities offered cooperation and / or coordination between group members.

2.6.1 Buyer power

1.) Many small customers acting as a group can create a strong force[45]

Supplier power

2.6.2 Importance of volume to supplier:[46] If the Industry is a important customer,suppliers' fortunes will be closely tied to the Industry and they will want to protect it through reasonable pricing and assistance in activities like R & D and lobbying.

Threat of Rivalry

2.6.3 Diverse Competitors[47]

Competitors diverse in strategies, origins, personalities, and relationships to their parent companies have different goals and differing strategies for how to compete and may continually run head on into each other in the process.

---

[45] Cloe ehmke, Joan Fulton, and Jay Akridge Pg 4
[46] Porter 1980 Pg 27
[47] Porter 1980 Pg 19

Threat of substitutes

2.6.4 Switching cost[48] It is easy for customers to switch

Barrier to entry

2.6.5 Economics of scale[49]: Economics of scale refer to declines in unit costs of a products the absolute volume per period increases. Economics of scale deter entry by forcing the entrant to come in at large scale and risk strong reaction from existing firms or come in at small scale and risk strong reaction from existing firms or come in at a small scale and accept cost disadvantage both undesirable options.

2.6.5.1 Product breadth[50]: The benefit of sharing are particularly potent if there are joint costs. Joint costs occur when a firm producing Product A must inherently have the capacity to produce product B.

2.7 Expressive or symbolic attributes[51]: The consumption of a product may have a symbolic connotations.e.g., a consumption may express status, exclusiveness, distinction, "savoir vivre", progressiveness, thrift, sobriety or modesty in consuming specific food items. These symbolic aspects may be important

---

[48] Cloe ehmke, Joan Fulton, and Jay Akridge Pg 10
[49] Porter 1980 Pg 7
[50] Porter 1980 Pg 9
[51] Wieranga,B 1983 Pg 127

to the consumer himself or may be meant to convey something about the consumer to persons in his social environment.

Barrier to entry

2.7.1 Market Breadth[52]:

A common situation of joint costs occurs when business units share intangible assets such as brand names and know-how. The cost of creating an intangible asset need only be borne once; the asset may then be freely applied to other businesses, subject only to any costs of adopting or modifying it. Thus situations in which intangible assets are shared can lead to substantial economics.

2.7.2 Economics to vertical Integration[53] operating in successive stages of production or distribution. Here the entrant must enter integrated or face a cost disadvantage, as well as possible foreclosure of inputs or markets for its product if most established competitors are integrated.

Fore closure in such situations stems from the fact that most customers purchase from in—house units, or most suppliers "sell" their inputs in house. The Independent firm faces a difficult time in getting comparable prices and may become "squeezed" if integrated competitors offer different terms

---

[52] Porter:1980 Pg 9
[53] Porter:1980 Pg 9

to it than to their captive units. The requirement to enter integrated may heighten the risk of retaliation.

3.0 Link between scope dimensions and Strategic posture: The PIMS-based research has established relationship among product breadth, market and performance and point to the importance of domain choice in general[54].

Strategic Repositioning through economics of scope.

3.1 Stage2: what benefits do the consumers[55] and /or buyers want?

A group of customers in one segment may belong to one product group and may have a opinion to go for a inexpensive substitute product. On the other hand the other group of customers in the other segment may feel that adding a few pennies will not make a difference to the existing cost. In the two above prospective customers respond to two different brands and they both do not respond to the same advertising claims.

3.1.1 Demand Perspective[56] considerations are expressly entertained by the focus on finding and satisfying the needs, tastes, and preferences of particular customer segments.

---

[54] Buzzell & Gale 1987 Pg 97-106
[55] Wieranga,1983 Pg 119-137
[56] Craig Fleischer & Barbara Bensoussan,2003 Pg 165

3.2 Benefit Segmentation[57]

Approach to market segmentation, whereby it is possible to identify market segments by causal factors rather than descriptive factors might be called "benefit segmentation". Their beliefs underlying this segmentation strategy is that the benefits which people are seeking in consuming a given product are the basic reasons for the existence of true market segments. Experience with this approach has shown that benefits sought by consumers determine their behaviour more accurately than do demographic characteristics or volume of consumption. This does not mean that the kinds of data gathered are more traditional types of segmentation are not useful. Once people have been classified into segments in accordance with the benefit they are seeking, each segment is contrasted with all of the other segments in terms of its demography, its volume of consumption, its brand perception, its media habits, its personality and lifestyle, and so forth. In this way, a reasonably deep understanding of the people who make up each segment can be obtained and by capitalising on this understanding, it is possible to reach them, to talk to them in their own terms, and to present a product in the most favourable light possible. This approach is based on being able to measure consumer value system in detail, together with what the consumer thinks about various brands in the market.

---

[57] Haley.R,1995 Pg 30-35

3.2.1 The method for employing the technique

Each segment is identified by the benefits it is seeking. However it is the total configuration of the benefits sought that differentiates one segment from another, rather than the fact that one segment is seeking one particular benefit and another a quite different benefit. Individual benefits are likely to have appeal for several segments. In fact, the research that has been done thus far suggests that most people would like as many benefits as possible. However, the relative importance they attach to individual benefits can differ importantly and, accordingly, can be used as an effective lever in segmenting markets.

3.3 Preference Weights indicating the importance of the different evaluative criteria in the determination of preferences: The evaluation criteria on attributes of choice are the dimensions of the product that play a role in the formation of preferences.

A consumer may attach great importance to product and attributes, but not price or it may be vice versa. This is reflected in the different weighting factors in his preference or utility function. These weights are closely related to motives, needs, personality factors, culture, social class, reference groups (family) etc. The evaluative criteria or attributes of choice are the dimensions of the product that play in the formation of preference,

Consumer's preference function[58]

3.4 Sensory evaluation function Toughness, succulence and flavour of the product

3.5 Instrumental and expressive attributes: packaging, brand etc may be a dominant influence on consumer choice. may be a consumer will not buy the most tasty product, but a product from a trusted brand or with a attractive packaging. Ultimately the preference function should incorporate all these different dimensions that affect consumer choice.

Barrier to entry:

3.5.1 Brand Identity[59]: products not unique or homogenous undifferentiated products compete mainly on price, because consumers receive the same value from the products of different firms. Because firms do not experience any insulation from price.

Supplier power

3.5.2 Differentiation of inputs[60] the input you require are available only from a small number of suppliers.

---

[58] Wieranga.B Pg 134
[59] Porter(1980), Pg 8 &14
[60] Cloe ehmke, Joan Fulton, and Jay Akridge Pg 2

3.5.2.1 Switching costs of suppliers and firms in the Industry[61]
The Inputs you require are unique, making it costly to switch suppliers.

3.5.2.2 Using Differentiation relative to supplier power[62]:
Differentiation yields higher margins with which to deal with supplier power. Reduces the buyer power, since buyers lack comparable alternatives and thereby less price sensitive. Competition, there is more likely to be active rivalry.

Threat of Rivalry

3.5.3 Brand Identity[63]
Where the product or service is perceived as commodity, choice by the buyer is largely based on price and service, and pressure for intense price and service competition result.

3.5.3.1 Product differences[64]
Creates layers of insulation against competitive war fare because buyers have preferences and loyalties to particular sellers.

3.5.3.2 Using differentiation relative to competitors[65]:
Differentiation provides insulation against competitive rivalry because of brand loyalty by customers and resulting low sensitivity to price. It also increases margins, which avoids the need for a low-cost position

---

[61] Cloe ehmke, Joan Fulton, and Jay Akridge Pg 2
[62] Porter 1980 Pg 19
[63] Porter 1980 Pg 19
[64] Porter 1980 Pg 19
[65] Porter 1980 Pg 19

Barrier to entry

3.5.4 Properitory Product differences[66] means that established firms have brand identification and customer loyalties, which stem from past advertising, customer service, product differences, or simply being first into the industry.

Differentiation creates a barrier to entry by forcing entrants to spend heavily to overcome existing brand. Brand name are particularly risky since they have no salvage value if entry fails customer loyalties. This effort usually involves start-up losses and often takes an extended period of time. Such investments in building.

3.6 Roadmapping[67] is the technique used by many companies, including high-tech firms such as Motorola to plan new product Development.

3.6.0.1 New Product Development[68]: When an organisation has successful products that are in the maturity stage of the PLC; he idea here is to attract satisfied customers to try new (improve) products as a result of their positive experience with the organisations present products or services. When an organisation competes in an industry that is characterised by rapid technological developments. When major competitors

---
[66] Porter 1980 Pg 9
[67] Will yard and McClees 1987 Pg 13-19,
[68] J.D Waldman, Strategic Management summer 2001 Pg 17

offer better quality products at comparable prices. When an organisation competes in a high growth industry.

Barrier to entry

3.6.1 Using Differentiation for Entry barriers[69] the resulting customer loyalty and the need for a competitor to overcome uniqueness provide entry barriers.

Buyer power

3.6.2 Buyer' switching cost relative to seller switching costs.[70] Switching costs lock the buyer to particular sellers.

3.6.2.1 Using differentiation relative to Buyers[71] Since Buyer lacks alternatives and is thereby fewer prices sensitive.

Threat of substitutes

3.6.3 Buyers propensity to substitute[72] : Substitute products are produced in Industry earning high profits. In such cases Substitutes often come rapidly into play if some developments increases competition in the industries causes price reduction or performance improvement.

3.6.3.1 Using Differentiation relative to substitutes[73] the firm that has differentiated itself achieves customer loyalty

---

[69] Porter 1980 Pg 38
[70] Porter 1980 Pg 25
[71] Porter 1980 Pg 38
[72] Porter 1980 Pg 24
[73] Porter 1980 Pg 38

should be better positioned vis-à-vis substitutes than its competitors.

The economic logic of Market segmentation analysis

3.6.3.2 The advantages of achieving customer value through economics of scope[74]

Firm's Customer value offering.	Rival's customer value offering
Customer value = $V_A(X) - P_X$ Where A = customer group X = characteristics of the firm's product P_X = price firm's product	Customer value = $V_A(Y) - P_Y$ Where A = customer group Y = characteristics of rival's product P_Y = price rival's product
Given that Y < X and PY < PX (i.e., product Y is inferior but also cheaper), consumers will buy product Y when the rival customer value offering exceeds the firm's customer value offering, or more formally when VA (Y)–PY.	

3.7 Attitude or utility[75]

The way the product is perceived in terms of the various attributes at one hand and the preference or utility weights on the other hand together determine the consumer's overall attitude to or utility for that product.

---

[74] Craig Fleisher &Barbette Bensoussen Pg 167
[75] Wieranga 1983 Pg 119-137

3.7.1 Fish bein–Rosenberg model[76]

$$A_b = \sum_{i=1}^{n} W_i B_{ib}$$

Ab = attitude toward alternative b
Wi = Weight or importance of evaluation criterion (i)
Bib = belief with respect to the ability of alternative b to satisfy evaluation criterion
(i) (i.e.) score of alternative "b" interims of attribute "i" n = number of salient attributes

3.8 Subsequent stages in the decision process.

The next stage in the choice process after alternative evaluation is the (4) Choice of course, normally one would expect a consumer to buy the alternatives he prefers the most (most favourable attitude). However, there may be a discrepancy between preference and choice. The attributes play a role in the determination of preferences and choice.

3.8.1 Choice–Attribute/cost Models of Customer Value[77]
one of the useful formal attribute models of customer value has been developed. The model views customer value as a combination of expected benefits and expected costs.

---

[76] Wieranga B 1983 Pg 126
[77] Craig Fleisher & Barbara Bensoussen, 2003 Pg 185

3.8.2 Expected Benefits are composed of product and service attributes1 which can further broken down into three categories of attributes that customer use to define benefits.

3.8.3 Presale attributes include the entire tangible product and search attributes that the customer can evaluate before the purchase. e.g., features of the product. Market premised on presale attributes will generally experience a high degree of price competition as many tangible attributes are easily imitated, eroding any source of competitive advantage through attribute differentiation.

3.8.4 Post sale attributes include the often intangible product and service attributes that can only be evaluated post sale after using the product or service for sometime.e.g. taste texture of a new brand. Extended post sale attributes include those products and services for which an evaluation of value can only be determined after extended usage. Markets based on post sale and extended post sale experience attributes offer a high chance of competitive advantage to those firms who successfully deliver superior experiences

3.8.5 Expected costs[78]
Customer value is the concept of expected costs which comprise three different types of cost:

- Transaction costs are the up-front cash costs or "sticker price" for the product or service.

---
[78] Craig Fleischer & Barbara Bensoussen,2003 Pg 186

Life cycle costs are the additional costs incurred by the customer over the total span of ownership of the product or service such as delivery, installation

- learning curves associated with initial usage, maintenance, repair, disposal, etc,
- Risk is the costs incurred by the customer when actual costs are higher than expected costs. Risk usually higher when the total span of ownership is long.
- Consumer choice is not only determined by the objective product attributes, but also by the way these attributes are perceived by the consumers. The perceptual filter indicates that in the perception process stimuli may be stored in the consumer memory in a biased way. False properties may be attributed to products. The attribute perceptions are, so to speak, the inputs to the process of preference formation. Through the preference or utility function of the consumer. The attribute perceptions are converted into attitude or utility ratings. filter indicates that in the perception process stimuli may be stored in the consumer memory in a biased way. False properties may be attributed to products. The attribute perceptions are, so to speak, the inputs to the process of preference formation. Through the preference or utility function of the consumer the attribute perceptions are converted into attitude or utility ratings

3.8.6 Model and Measurement methodology for the analysis of consumer choice

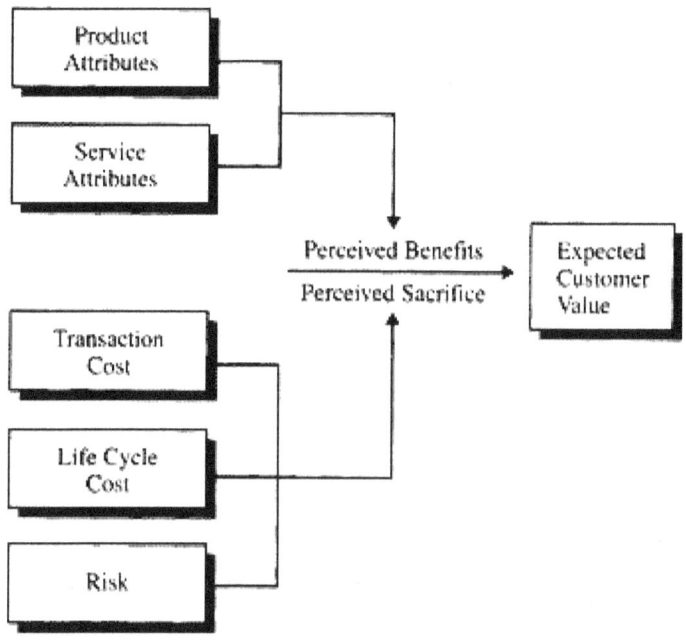

3.8.7 Outcome[79] after an alternative has been chosen, it is consumed, which results in a certain outcome. The product may or may not live to expectations. The experience constitutes a feedback loop and experience is updated. Transaction costs have the most influence on the purchase decision in commodity markets in which products have short life spans. For products and services with long life span, life cycle costs, and risk are more important

---

[79] Wieranga, 1983 Pg 119-137

Reference Books

1. Buzzell, Robert D, and Bradley T.Gale 1987 PIMS principle, New York. Free press
2. Bolman, L.G and T.Deal, 1997. Reframing Organisations Artistry, choice, and leadership, 2nd edition, San Franscisco, CA Jossey-Das Publishers
3. Camp, R. 1989, Benchmarking: the search for industry best practices that lead to superior performance. Quality press. Milwaukee, Wisconsin
4. Craig S. Fleischer & Barbette E. Bensoussen. Strategy and Competitor analysis
5. FINKELSTEIN, S. & HAMBRICK, D.1996. Strategic leadership: top executives and their effects on organisations. West Publishing Company Minneapolis
6. Grinyer, P.H & Norburn, D 1977/1978. "Planning for existing markets. An empirical study". International studies in Management and Organisation Vol 17 pp.99-122
7. Hall, William K.1980, 2 Survival strategies in a hostile environment, "Harvard Business Review" (September-October), Pg 75–85
8. Mintzberg, Henry, B.Ahlstrand, and J.Lampel.1998 Strategy safari: A Guided tour through the wilds of strategic Management. New York, NY The free press
9. Porter M.E., 1985 Competitive advantage: creating and sustaining performance

10. Porter M.E., 1985 Competitive advantage: creating and sustaining performance
11. Porter M.E. Competitive advantage, New York Press. 1980
12. Porter M.E 1979. The structure within Industries and companies performance. Review of economics and statistics May. 214-227
13. Sanchez & Heene,A,1996. A sytems theory of the firm in competence-based competition. In Sanchez:Heene & Thomas,1996,Pg 39-62
14. Snuif, H.R, and P.S Zwart(1994 a) Strategische besluitvorming in net MKB: Een process model,MAB,mci Pp 264-274
15. The new Competitive Intelligence, the complete resource for finding and analysing . . . by Leonard M.Fuld, Fuld & Company, Cambridge, MA
16. Thompson J.D, 1967, Organisations in action New York. McGraw Hill
17. Volberda, H.W, and T.Elfring, 2001.Rethinking strategy, London, sage publications
18. Porter M.E., 1985 Competitive advantage: creating and sustaining performance
19. Porter M.E. Competitive advantage, New York Press. 1980
20. Porter M.E 1979. The structure within Industries and companies performance. Review of economics and statistics May. 214-227

21. The new Competitive Intelligence, the complete resource for finding and analysing . . . by Leonard M.Fuld, Fuld & Company, Cambridge, MA
22. Thompson J.D, 1967, Organisations in action New York. McGraw Hill
23. Volberda, H.W, and T. Elfring, 2001. Rethinking strategy, London, sage publications

Journals

1. Ashton, B., & Sen R.K., 1988. Using Patent information in technology and business planning I. "Research Technology Management", 31 (69) Pg 42-46
2. Beal,R.M(2000),Competingefficiently:environmental scanning competitive strategy and organisational Performance in small Manufacturing firm, Journal of small Business Mangement, Vol 38(1), Pp27-47
3. Bradley, Robert D., and Bradley T. Gale and Ralph G.M. Sultan, 1975 "Market share-A key to Profitability", HBR, 53 (January/February), Pg 97-106.
4. Brandenburger, Adam M, and Barry J.Nelebuff.1995. The Right game: use Game theory to shape strategy. Harvard business Review July-August: 57-71
5. Gilinsky, E Stanny, R.L McLine and R. Eyler (2001). Does firm size matter? An empirical investigation into the competitive strategies of the small firm. Journal of Small Business Strategy, Vol 12(20 Pp 1-11

6. Gray, J.H (1997),small business strategy in Australia, Academy of Entrepreneurship Journal,Vol 2(2). Pp 44-58
7. Haley, R., 1968. Benefit Segmentation: A decision oriented research tool. Journal of Marketing July, Vol 32, pp 30-35
8. Hamel & Prahlad, 1991 corporate imagination and expeditionary Marketing
9. Hitt, M.A., R.D. Ireland, S.M. Camp and D.L. Sexton, 2001 Strategic entrepreneurship: Entrepreneurial strategies for wealth creation. Strategic Management Journal 22 (Special issue). Pg 479.491
10. Hoouthoofd, N, & Heene, A 1997: Strategic groups as subsets of strategic scope groups in the Belgian brewing Industry Strategic Management studies July Pg 429-451
11. HAMBRICK, D.C., 1982. Environmental scanning and organisational Strategy Strategic Management Journal Vol 3 Pg 159-174
12. Lawrence C.Rhyne, Mary B.Teagarten, William Van den Panhuyzen. Journal of High technology Management Research.Dept of Management, College of Business Administration. San Diego State University,San Diego, A 92182
13. KEFLAS, A & SCHOLERBEK, P.P., 1973. Scanning the business environment some empirical results, Decision Sciences Vol. 4, Pg 63-74

14. Karki, M.M.S., 1997. "Patent Citation analysis. A policy analysis tool. "World Patent information, 19(4), Pg 269-272
15. Montgomery, C.A., and M.E. Porter(eds): 1991 Strategy: seeking and securing competitive advantage: Boston, MA: Harvard Business School press.
16. MIntzberg, H (1994) Strategie vorming:tien scholen,Script im Management
17. Miller, D., & Friesen, P., 1977."Strategy making in context: Ten empirical archetypes, "Journal of Management studies, 14839, 253-280
18. Murphy, G.B, J.W. Trailer and R.C Hill (1996), Measuring performance in entrepreneurship research, Journal of Business Research, Vol 36, Pp 15-23
    Nelson, R.R., 1991. Why do firms differ, and how does it matter? Strategic Management Journal, 12-Pg 61-748 Winter Special Issue
19. Parker, A.R (2000) Impact on the organisational performance of the strategy technology policy interaction, Journal of Business research, Vol.47 Pp 55-64.
20. Pelham, A.M (2000), Market orientation and other potential influences on Performance in small and medium-sized manufacturing firms, Journal of small business Management, Vol 38(1), Pp 48-67.
21. Porter M.E (1991),Towards a dynamic theory of strategy,Strategic Management Journal,Vol 12.Pp 95-117.

22. 22. Postma, T.J.B.M. and D.S. Zwart, 2001, Strategic research and performance of SMEs Journal of small business strategy, Vol. 1292 Pg 52-64
23. 23. Sanchez,R: Heene, A, & Thomas H (1996). Dynamics of Competence—based competition:Theory and practice in the nem strategic Management
24. 24. Sanchez & Heene,A(1997) Reinventing strategic management: new theory and practice for competence-based competition. European Management Journal,Vol 15, No 3. PP.303-317
25. 25. Snuif,H.R, and P.S Zwart (1994a) Strategische Besluitvorming in net MKB: Een process model, MAB, mci Pp 264-274 20. issue)
26. 26. SIMON, H.A., 1967."Motivational and emotional controls of cognition", Psychological Review, 74, Pg 29-39
27. 27. Wieranga, B., 1983. Model and measurement methodology for the analysis of consumer choice for food products, Journal of food quality no.6, Pg 119-137

Working paper

1. Marylyn Placet and Kristi.M.Branch Chapter 3 version 2.doc,06.08.02
2. Willyard, C.H., and C.W. McClees, 1987. Motorola Technology Roadmap process research Management Sept/Oct, Pg 13-19

3. Research Report: Strategy and small performance P.Gibcus, R.G.M. Kemp. Zoetermeer, January 2003

Internet sources

1. Industry analysis — CSA5eCO3 (1).PDF
2. WP data/IPCWEB/MSWORD/WP-9MS.Doc., March 1994
3. J.D. Waldman Strategic Management Anderson 598 Summer 2001 Pg 20
4. Houthoofd and Heene, A systems view on what matters to excel. May 2000, Pg 22.
5. AICC Purdue University Purdue University Agricultural Innovation and Commercialisation Center, Industry Analysis; the five forces, 2002
6. www.sbaer.uca.edu/research/2000/swma/Doswma63.htm 2002, Pg 1-11

Abbreviations

RBV . . . . Resource Based View
MIS . . . . Marketing Information Systems

Illustrations

Figure 1 . . . Environmental Scanning to supply and apply strategy
Figure 2 . . . Identifiable steps in Competitive Intelligence Gathering
Figure 3 . . . Example of SWOT analysis of company A
Figure 4 . . . Types of methods on how companies compete
Figure 5 . . . Example of data through Internet Intelligence
Figure 6 . . . Example of Patent citation of Hitachi
Figure 7 . . . Steps on Environmental scan
Figure 8 . . . The five forces shaping strategy
Figure 9 . . . Strategic positioning
Figure 10 . . . . A model for the choice of Food product
Figure 11 . . . . Attribute Cost model of Customer Value

www.ingramcontent.com/pod-product-compliance
Lightning Source LLC
Chambersburg PA
CBHW021043180526
45163CB00005B/2262